When Sin Really Hits the Church

Picking up the Broken Pieces

LeTasha S. Robinson

Foreward By

Overseer Constance White

All Scripture quotations are taken from the King James Version unless otherwise indicated.

All definitions were obtained from Merriam-Webster online unless otherwise indicated.

ISBN 978-0-69244740-6
Copyright © 2015 by LeTasha S. Robinson
P.O. Box 15
Lexington, South Carolina 29071

Other Books by *LeTasha S. Robinson*

When Life Gives You Lemons (2015)
How Well Do you Tip (Coming in 2016)
Can I get in the funeral Car Please (Coming in 2016)

Contact Information

LeTasha Robinson
PO Box 15
Lexington, SC 29071

Email: Lsrobins@yahoo.com

 L Robinson

 LSROBINSON

Dedication and Thanks

This book is dedicated to the man that has been consistent in my life. He has never left me nor forsaken me. He is my friend, my father, and my leader; my Heavenly Father. I love this man more and more with each passing day. He has inspired and encouraged me to finish this book. I give him all praise and honor for without him there would be no me.

To both my natural and spiritual family I so appreciate how you have assisted me with my growth. To the greatest church on this side of Heaven (in my opinion) Zion Hopewell under the leadership of Bishop and Elder White. How you have held my hand and comforted me during many times on this journey. I am a Zionite! My mom and dad the Seibles I luv you more! I thank God for you all and pray that He bless you tremendously.

To three friends that has been with me since the early years of my life. Yolonda, Cicely, and Olandra. You have held my hands during the worst and best times of my life. To have you in my life has truly been a blessing.

To the editors of the book Vanessa and Keia you two made this book possible. I thank the both of your for your patience and your kindness when it came to editing this book. You two are truly a gift from God.

Finally, this book is dedicated to all of those who need to know that where you are currently isn't your forever. God created you with a purpose in mind and I pray that you will learn to walk in it fully regardless of who stays and who doesn't.

Foreword

This book *When Sin Really Hits the Church,* will challenge the reader's mindset to be different. *Romans 12:1,2* KJV I beseech you therefore, brethren, by the mercies of God, that you present your bodies a living sacrifice, holy, acceptable to God, which is your reasonable services.

And do not be conformed to this world, but be transformed by the renewing of your mind, that you may prove what is that good and acceptable and perfect will of God. To those who will read this book it is not to be taken for granted. It will cause you to seek God with all of your heart.

Psalms 42:1 KJV As the deer pants for the water brooks, so pants my soul for you O God. It will cause you to seek God to reset your mind and your heart.

Overseer Constance White

Table of Contents

Dedications

Foreword

Introduction

Introduction

I started writing this book in 2012. However, I didn't finish it until 2013. The year 2012 was a hard year for me. I went from being financially stabled, to sleeping on someone's couch for nine months. I went from having everything, to calling and begging my creditors to give me a little more time. Of all that I've gone through, the most tragic event happened on November 7, 2012 when I lost my sister. This book was finished through the pain and hurt that came from watching my sister take her last breath.

As I lay in bed asleep, suddenly I became wide awake. I looked at the clock that read Tuesday, January 21, 2014, 4:01 AM. I laid there and said, *"God speak for your servant hears thee"*. He said it was time. Closing my eyes, I held back the tears because I knew exactly what He was talking about.

This book deals with the "un-forgiveness" and how not dealing with it affects your life.

~November 2012~

I had stayed up all night watching the election. As the numbers became final, I dozed off excited, not knowing in just a few hours, my excitement and my tears of joy would become heartache, despair, and desperation before I could get out of the door. In just a few more hours, my world would forever change. One of my older sisters called me and said that our sister had taken a turn for the worse and the doctors weren't expecting her to live.

Getting off that phone, the tears started to flow. The last time that I had spoken to my sister, we'd gotten into a bad argument. We didn't speak to each other for months and now, here I stood getting a phone call saying she was about to pass. I became delirious with hurt and regret. She and I were both stubborn and neither one would call the other one. All that time wasted and now here I was, standing with a heart full of regret, praying to God to give us a little more time so that I could make this right. I was standing and praying that God would honor my request and do as he did with Hezekiah and add more years to her life. I got dressed as fast as I could not know what to expect when I entered my sister's hospital room.

I got to the hospital and immediately I saw my family. Sitting in the downstairs lobby, they told me where she was. I went up to her room and opened the door. I had never seen my sister in pain or quiet.

I was expecting to walk through the door and hear how God had turned it all around and to hear her say something but that is not what met me. I stood there, looking at her. Then I went to the side of her bed and began to hold her hands and rub them to keep them warm. In my heart, I was screaming, "I'm sorry. Please forgive me for being so stubborn." I remember saying in my head, "If you forgive me, squeeze my hand." I sat there and all of a sudden, she started squeezing my hand with what little strength she had. She heard my heart cry and as the decision was made.

Hospice came in to make her comfortable. I stood outside of her room waiting, until hospice left and I entered again. In my heart, I knew this would be the last time I would see my sister alive. I played with her hair and touched her face and apologized for being so bull-headed for allowing so much time to pass without speaking to her. I got off of that bed as the tears began to flow and started towards the door when I heard, "Come here." I turned around and saw my sister sitting up in bed right hand extended, telling me to come to her. With barely enough strength to keep her head lifted, she asked me to 'come to here' again. I knew that it had to be God because she'd lay in that same bed, unresponsive for most of the day, unless she was screaming out in pain. I went and sat on the bed and stared at her and said, "I Love You." She stared back, smiled, and said, "I love you too." All of a sudden, she fell in my arms. We hugged each other as long as we could. She finally sat up and laid back and said, "Now let me go." Thirty minutes later, I walked back into her room and she looked at me and smiled as her eyes began to close for the last time; while she took her last breath.

After realizing this was it, the tears started to flow. My sister passed and I stood there looking at her lifeless body. My strength came. I went to straighten her up in bed and closed her eyes. Sitting by the bed, I became consumed with guilt for not being there sooner. If I had only listened to the Holy Spirit and put it all aside. But no, I wanted to hold on to hurt and pain. All I could do was wish that I had at least five more minutes. I can never make up for the time that I lost while being angry with my sister for something that could have been so easily forgotten and more importantly forgiven. I kept saying, I'll do it later but my later kept becoming further and further away until it was almost too late. Forgiveness in this Life is necessary. This book was finished out of the pain and hurt that I experienced that day. Regretting moments that were not spent with her because of the bitterness and anger that consumed me. I cannot go back and change the time but I can hopefully make you look and rethink situations that you are thinking about holding onto.

This book was written to assist those who are dealing with "un-forgiveness" to learn how to set yourself free. It is better to have loved than to not have loved at all is what the world says, but I say it is better to forgive then not to forgive. Forgiveness is for you. When you forgive those who have hurt you, you regain power over your life. This book is my journey on learning how to forgive others but most importantly, myself. I saw what "un-forgiveness" almost cost me. Now all I have left are the memories of that day and how my sister fell into my arms. It was almost as though at that moment, as we held each other, we were quietly telling each other that we were sorry for the time not spent.

On this walk called life, many have been fooled thinking since God is using them, that they are good. But if God used a donkey, He will use you also. Being used by God isn't an indication that you have your act together. It is just an indication that you were willing to submit to him. You can still be used by God and still miss it. At the end of the day when you are not being blessed as you should and you ask yourself why? I can tell you why. It is called S-I-N. God can't bless what isn't right. So if you are tired of living the mediocre life that you are in; if you are tired of being sick and tired, then, this book is for you. Through my pain, sweat, and tears, this book was born. I pray it impacts your life just as much, if not more, than it has impacted me writing it. Now take the Journey with Me!

Sincerely,
LeTasha S. Robinson

There aren't any dead ends in life.

L. Robinson

Chapter One

What is the Church?

When people say the word 'church,' many people think about the actual building. The church, for centuries, has been symbolized by a building. However, that is not the case. In the book of Acts, Jesus departed the earth so that the comforter could come to us. The comforter, who is the Holy Spirit, came and was imparted to us by the Baptism of Fire and with the evidence of speaking in tongue.

It was at that point, that the Holy Spirit no longer resided in a building or in the Ark of the Covenant. We became the residing place of the Holy Spirit. We became the House or what many people call "the church." From the death, burial, and resurrection, the Holy Spirit was designed to take us back to how Adam and Eve were in the Garden of Eden. A place where God could be in constant communion with us, as we walked as one with him speaking his very heart.

Adam walked with God in the cool of the day (Genesis 3). He communed with God throughout the day. He walked, talked, and acted like God until one day, all of that was taken away from him. On that day, the Holy Spirit could no longer reside in a temple with sin. On that day, the Holy Spirit departed from us to only be brought back by the slaying of an innocent lamb called Jesus! Jesus restored to us what had been taken. We were restored with the ability to commune with him on a daily basis through the indwelling of the Holy Spirit.

The Bible describes the Holy Spirit as a comforter, one that will guide you. For example, have you ever had that moment where you were inconsolable about a certain situation and after speaking in tongues or praying about it, it seems as though you had peace about that situation? The situation may still look the same in the physical but now you are comforted knowing that you are not alone and that now someone is there to help lighten your load? Well, if you have ever felt like that, then you have been touched by the Holy Spirit. Maybe you've felt like 'something' was telling you not to do something or go another way. That 'something' is the Holy Spirit.

The Holy Spirit dwells in us all and not in a building. The building is necessary but we are the Church. The Bible states in both Ephesians and I Corinthians that He will use some evangelists, teachers, pastors, prophets, and apostles for the perfecting of the Body of Christ. These offices cannot help a building because it is not alive, however these gifts can help us as a people. We need an evangelist to help lead us to Christ and to learn how we can be comforted by Christ. We need the teacher to help us with laying the foundation of the new life. We need a Pastor to help lead us and feed us the word from Heaven. The Prophet comes to point us in the right direction and the Apostle helps bring unity and set up churches within the community that are designed to help bring out our gifts. These gifts are not for a building, but for the perfecting of the church which is us.

So what happens when sin really hits the church? How do we respond? How do we deal with it? Do we do like most people and cover it up with a bandage? What happens when sin get to a point where you can no longer cover it up or ignore it because it's at the surgical stage? This is where I was, before I started writing this book. I had gone through challenge after challenge. I had lost sight of what God had called me to do. I was hurting in ways that I could not begin to explain and didn't know how to deal with the hurt. Yes, I was in church every time the church doors opened. I was working and working because I thought that was what saints were supposed to do. I was hanging on the old fool's tale that as long as I was working in the church, everything will be fine. How dumb was I to think that going to a building would solve all of my problems? I had fooled myself into thinking that as long as I was in the church I would be ok. The word was coming forth but I was not applying it. The church soon became a life support mechanism for me. I

3

would walk through the doors of the church and put on my mask. "Good Morning, Praise the Lord, I am Blessed, Isn't the Lord Good?" These are the familiar church clichés that I had become accustomed to saying because I couldn't let anyone know what was going on with me. What would they think, how would they treat me after they learned my secrets? How will they look at me if they see me walking to the front of the church for prayer?

I made the decision for years, to hide behind a ton of work instead of dealing with my own issues. I would just work and work and pretend. In my mind, I figured if I keep doing something over and over again everything would be alright? That is what I thought. Little did I know that the transformation had to start on the inside of me in order to affect anyone or anything around me. God will use you but that doesn't mean that you are necessarily in line to receive His blessings. Being used by God isn't an indication that you have yourself; so together that you can withstand the simplest of tests. Being used by God only indicates that at that point where you were a willing vessel. You can be used and after being used, go right back to the depressed or oppressed state that you were in before.

I am the church and when sin hit me, I didn't know how to deal with it. So what happens when sin really hits the church? Where is the love for the fallen angel? Can you look in the mirror and love yourself or do you look in the mirror and see self-hatred for things that were beyond your control? Do you blame yourself and feel as though you could have prevented it? Well, let's take a journey to see what happens when SIN REALLY HITS THE CHURCH!

Stop storing up treasures for yourselves on earth, where moths and rust destroy and where thieves break in and steal. But keep on storing up treasures for yourselves in heaven, where moths and rust do not destroy and where thieves do not break in and steal, because where your treasure is, there your heart will be also.

Matthew 6: 19-21

Chapter Two

An Over Worked Heart

Sin has many different definitions. Most think that sin is doing something wrong, such as having sex before marriage, getting drunk, stealing, etc. but what is sin really? I like to consider that sin is anything that blocks you from having full communication with God. So, if we take that into consideration, sin can be a feeling, a thought, or even an act. Too often we as believers walk around with a sin-filled heart, holding on to the thoughts of what happened yesterday; he left me, I was raped, or I never felt loved. We've walked down this road called life, never really learning how to deal with the difficulties that life can bring and how to overcome tragic moments.

As believers, we aren't supposed to celebrate Halloween. Yet, there are many that walks around with masks on every day. Instead of dealing with the hurt and pain of what happened they sweep it under the rug and choose to deal with it later. However, as time goes on, later never comes until one day that the bump under your rug is so large that it can no longer cover your issues. What was thought was cleverly covered, is now uncovered. You may be the one that people have to walk softly around because no one knows what will tick you off that day. You may be the one who is always the victim and you are never wrong. Guess what? Somewhere, you have made the decision not to forgive and it is causing you to act in ways that are not of God. You have hidden behind the lies that lay under the rug and reacting to each and every bump. It only takes a second to change your life as you know it.

When we get to the church, we live with the infamous lie that "someone has it worse than me." We constantly sweep how we feel and the pain of it, under the gigantic rug that lies over the rips and torn pieces of our hearts. We then wonder why the onset of heart disease is on the rise. Could it be because we are dealing

7

with a wounded heart emotionally and spiritually? That we allow the fatty toxins of unforgiveness, hate, lies, bitterness, and other unhealthy feelings to clog our arteries to the point that our heart can no longer handle the load and just stops beating? In order to have a healthy heart, we must allow it to exercise all parts and not just some parts. When parts of our body are not in use for long periods of time, we find ourselves in a place where that one bad part can be the deadly blow to our way of life. When the heart is not functioning properly, this causes the unused parts to put a strain on the working parts, causing them to work harder to support the entire body. Can you imagine carrying an extra 200 pounds around every day or another living body that you cannot separate yourself from? This additional 200 pounds or person is attached to your body. It has its own heartbeat, its own thoughts, its on everything. The only problem is that its total survival is dependent upon you. Almost like a tick on an animal; if you die, they die. If you cannot fathom such a thought, then why do we do it to our hearts?

We make our hearts do unnecessary work because we hold on to unnecessary stuff. We can't forget or forgive. Have you ever heard the saying "I will forgive but I will never forget?" We allow the memories of what happened yesterday to constantly burden us. Those memories are constantly replayed over and over in our minds, bodies, our hearts and souls. We just simply can't understand what is going on. We say we want to be free but yet we put chains over our hearts and minds with the words 'I won't be hurt like that again,' or 'I am going to repay them for what they did to me.' These words cause sin to enter into our body. Now our bodies have become places where we only allow certain people access to certain things. I have married friends who used to say that I am their best friend. I quickly correct them and tell them that their spouse should be their best friend. Your spouse should be your best friend. You lay with your spouse almost every night, with the exception of occasional travel. So the question becomes how can you lay with someone and still not trust them? It is easy and it is called SIN. The worse part of it is, we lay with the Holy Spirit in us every day. Yet, some of us still don't trust HIM!

We go through this life blaming others for our past mishaps. Yes, some things may have happened that were beyond your control. However, it is up to you to decide how long you will hold onto them.   Have you ever been rushing to get through an intersection while the light is yellow, but the person in front of you causes you to miss it? They make it through but you're stuck at the red light. Slamming on brakes and coming to a screeching halt, you stop and become angry and impatient. If only that person hadn't gotten in front of you causing you, to miss your opportunity to go. Much like the scenario with the yellow and red lights, you are ready to go but can't because it isn't your time to go. Your light is still red.   Isn't this similar to life? You find yourself stuck at or in a situation because of someone else's decision.

Chapter Three

Stuck at the Red Light

There are roads in life that all of us must travel. Some roads we choose to travel. While others are roads we do not. I don't know of many people who wake up with the idea, "Yes, I am going to be raped today or molested." Then I'll follow it up with being in several physical and mentally abusive relationships, and top if off by adding just a little of depression and oppression.

I don't think anyone would have chosen that path. I know I wouldn't, but yet that was part of my life-the road I travelled. For years, due to past relationships and past heartache and pain, I chose the path that I thought was right for me. I never dreamed that I would have to travel down some of these roads with the feeling that I wasn't worthy of living. I found myself crying many days; wondering why I was ever born. I found myself stuck at different red lights so many times; crying so hard that I could barely see and screaming at God. The questions were always the same. "Where do I go from here? Which way do I turn?' At times I was so distraught; I would finally find myself at a green light but wouldn't go because I couldn't see through the tears. I would hear the sound of the horns of other cars blowing, letting me know that I was preventing them from reaching their destination because of my inability to see my own.

This is what happens when you allow unforgiveness to come into your heart and reside there. You are at a place where you want to move but fear keeps you stationary. You stay there ignoring the signs around you telling you that it is time to go. You are afraid that you may get hurt again, or that a situation may arise that you wouldn't be able to control. You sit there at that light holding everyone else up because of your lack of forgiveness. Forgiveness is for you and not the other person. You were running the race then something happened, and they passed you and now you are sitting at a red light. You are left with the memories of how that person just left you as though nothing happened. It didn't stop them and where they were going. Yet, you are motionless, and wondering and asking, "God, why did this happen to me?"

You want to move but you can't. Many times we arrive at road blocks in life and it forces us to stop and review the path that we are travelling. We don't have a choice. We are stuck and left to look at the scenery before us as well as what's behind us. Many times, it's what is behind us that we are trying to outrun. The question then becomes what happens when you can't run anymore? Your past has caught up with you and you can't run from it anymore. You find yourself at a point where you can either break the law by running the red light or find the purpose for your pain and grow from it. God wants you to be free from the troubling things of your past. The process of becoming free has to be one that you really want and a task that you are ready to endure.

Sometimes when you're at the red light there's nothing to do but to look around and face a future where you are limited to see or to face a past that is so easy to remember. Having to deal with the unknown, can make going back to the old ways of doing things seem like the right thing to do. We don't want to deal with who has hurt us or who walked out on us. However, we find that it's ok to drink enough alcohol to make us forget it for the moment or continue to participate in unsavory activities such as having sex with different people. That was my life. I constantly found myself getting stuck at one red light after another. Every time I thought that I was about to break through, here came another obstacle. That car which was no longer in view has moved on. Yet, here I was, still stuck at the place where they left me. The people who hurt us have moved on and left us. We are still left with the regrets, the pain, the memories, and trying to get back on the right track or back on the road. You are stuck at the red light looking at the tail lights of the other cars, while having to deal with the mess that you have made for yourself.

11

When I look back at my life as previous mentioned, I often found myself at many red lights crying. I can remember at least three times because of my inability to see, when I ran off the road and almost killed myself. The hurt was so bad that I just didn't want to live anymore and guess what? I was saved and in the church raising my hands every Sunday praising God and walking back out of the church the same way I had came in; sometimes worse because I didn't take my problems to God. I didn't take them to God but I wanted someone to physically see what was going on with me; the look of depression, the you don't praise God like you use to voice, or you were crying out in church so much that you expect someone to say "What is going on" or "You was in my SPIRIT!" How often has this happened and then when someone finally does ask you what is going on you say 'NOTHING.' I laugh to myself now how my inward cry of needing and wanting help but the outward pride that wouldn't allow me to admit I needed help. "No I am fine," "I'm OK" are words that I would utter while the weight of the world was steadily increasing. Finally, my doctor told me that I needed to be put on high blood pressure medicine because my heart was straining so hard to try to push blood through my veins to the other parts of my body. My heart was simply being overworked. The fat had built up and was causing other health issues that were overworking my heart.

Too many of us are stuck at the red light and don't know where to go. Some of us have been stuck at the same red light for over years and don't even realize that everything around us has changed and everything around us is still moving. Others have gone on with life and accepted the changes and we are still stuck at the same red light remembering what happened not realizing that the light has turned green; a couple of times. Our inability to move is preventing others from moving on.

When people are hurt, many times they stop where they were hurt at and blame that person or blame God. Someone else is the cause for you being stuck at that moment. Someone else is the cause and they are going to pay. You are never going to talk to them again. You are going to find a way to hurt them and anyone or anything else that looks like them. Yep, that was me. However, the problem was that I kept finding myself stuck at too many red lights. For every person who hurt me, I stopped and stayed at the red light; unable to move. One day, I looked in my rearview mirror and saw a line of cars that were all waiting on me to MOVE. Yet another problem had crept up on me; I didn't know how to move. They were blowing the horn, yelling out of the window, banging on the steering wheels but I still couldn't move. I had been stuck at the same place for so long that I couldn't remember what to do next. It was causing the people behind me to suffer and to miss their own appointments with destiny.

The world tells us to get back at a person; while God says vengeance is His (Romans 12:19). When we take things into our own hands, we make matters worse. We stress ourselves out trying to be right, and trying not to talk to a particular person. We lose energy by trying to avoid a situation instead of just facing it head on. We live a lie that everything is OK, it won't happen again, or I'm ok. Many times, people wait until they break completely down and it is at their breakdown that they realize it wasn't just affecting them but everyone around them. They think that they have to be strong and that they can do it all; all by themselves. All of this knowledge and inability to ask for help, will cause you to be in a place of war; constantly debating what to do. Do you do as the world would have you do seeking revenge or do you do as God would have you to do and forgive?

When you feel as though you have to protect yourself, you will always be insecure in your calling and in the things that you are trying to do in life. Insecure people always have to be in control. They don't have the ability to live life on the edge or to allow mistakes to happen, these people are emotionally unstable in many of their ways. I have found that trying to do it all by myself has caused me to lose my peace. There is no amount of money that you could give me for my peace. I used to walk around paranoid about who would hurt me next. In order to prevent that, I became a hard shell-of-a woman in order to protect myself. I was mean and nasty but then would cry and wonder why people didn't like me. I felt that if someone really wanted to be in my life, they would see beyond the hardened exterior to the little girl inside crying out. When people didn't see that little girl, I made it a law that people never meant me any good. Because of this mentality, I have destroyed a lot of friendships and had to fight off a lot of depression and suicidal thoughts growing up thinking that the world would be better off without me.

God never meant for you to be heavy burdened with worry and anxiety. He wants you to be abundantly free. However, if we are constantly tying ourselves up with the worries of the world, we will never experience this life. We will be too concerned about what others think about us, never seeking to hear from the Master himself. He so loved the world that He gave his only begotten Son (John 3:16). The key word in this scripture is 'gave.' Love is an action word. Without action, it is just a word with no purpose. God didn't just love us. He wanted the ability to commune with us on a daily basis so he sent His only begotten Son to teach, and to perform miracles on those who had been in bondage for years. He healed, delivered, and anointed those to be Apostle. He bore our sickness, took on the beatings, and then hung His head and died; just to demonstrate that he loves us. Jesus' entire life was to show us that God loves us unconditionally.

Before I started walking this path out, I became pregnant at the age of 18. I was in my freshman year of college at Benedict College. I thank God for my alma mater because they had a support system in place. I thank God for that because it was this support system that allowed me overcome this moment in my life. When I found out that I was pregnant, they immediately assisted me with getting in a program to help me prepare for all that came with becoming a new mother. Unfortunately, on December 23, 1999, I lost my baby. I remembered being in a daze that entire time. It was two days before Christmas and five days before my birthday. I can even recall not going to church for two years because of everything that had happened. I felt that God had turned his back on me. Instead of facing the fact that there were other issues which led me to having a miscarriage, I immediately blamed God. I didn't consider any other contributing factors that lead to my miscarriage. Once again, I was blinded by the hurt and the pain of my situation, and it made me unable to see the truth so that I could deal with the situation correctly. I went back to school trying to just be a robot. When one of the counselors pulled me to the side and asked me what was wrong. After seating in her office and not saying anything she started asking questions and that is when the water works started. I started telling her, that I had happened and how I lost my child. That day she put me in contact with a counselor. I was able to go to counseling for free. I am forever grateful to Benedict because if it wasn't for the constant prodding of my professors and the staff there I would not be the woman that I am today.

The counselor assisted me with giving me principles to get over the miscarriage of my child but then the overwhelming amount of shame started to rear its ugly head and up to a couple of years of ago was winning the battle. When I started working on this book, I stopped several times because the Spirit of Shame came over me. Just the mere thought of finishing this book made me want to run. How could I tell others things that in my opinion, were too private to share? I mean, how would people react if they knew the truth about why I was constantly in church or why I was always running to get prayed for? The Spirit of Shame was consuming me and I started doing everything else but finishing this book. For months, I allowed it to lay dormant. One day, after a day spent in worship, I felt an urgency to start the book again. The bulk of this book was written in those three days. The pieces of the puzzle started coming together and my fingers continued to pour out the matters of my heart until I felt a peace and I knew it was complete.

When sin hits you, the Spirit of Shame whispers to you that no one wants to hear what you have to say and you begin to fear how people will look at you after they've found out your truths? Well, I am at a point in my life where I look back and realize that I have always been labeled as peculiar. I have been talked about every day of my life; whether it was good, bad or indecent, but I AM STILL HERE. I am still here to give them something else to talk about. It's unto the Glory of GOD. More importantly, I want to be able to hear God say, "I am well pleased." Every time God told me to work on this book and I didn't move, I feel as if I moved myself a little further from the destiny that He has in store for me. Every time I procrastinated and did something else, I became separated from the purpose that would be birthed out through my pain. Every time...well the bus stops here and I choose take control of the reins of my destiny and say let's go!

Chapter Four

Escaping the Heartache of the Past or Was I?

Often times we find ourselves still stuck at the red light; tired and aggravated because precious time has been wasted. Why haven't the light changed? It seems as though everyone is passing you by and all you can think of is the person that made you get stuck at the red light. Angrily, you start to slam your hands on the steering wheel and mumble under your breath because you felt like you were given the short end of the stick. The person ahead of you should be there stuck at the light too. How did they make it through the light and not me? That's not fair God! Why does it seems like the ones who hurt us get off scot free and we're left stuck. Why God, why!

Where is the American's Dream that they talk about on TV? Why does it always seem as though the things that I want and I desire are so far off? Ok, I get it. I must be in a nightmare, a nightmare called LIFE! Why can't what I want just happen without any backlash? Is my life ordained to be filled with so many little ideas of hope to just be crushed and blown away? Have you ever felt like that? I know growing up this, was my motto-destined to be doomed. I put myself so far down that I saw and felt as though I had no value; worthless. I didn't want to live. I thought I was just taking up space on Earth that someone who was actually wanted or loved could have taken up. I mean who would want me if my own parents didn't want me?

As I sit back and reminisce while writing this book, I remember how dreadful I felt all the time. The glass was never half full. In fact, the glass was totally empty with no hope of ever being filled again. I had voids in my life and I didn't understand what they were or how to get them filled. I wanted so badly to be loved and accepted. I dreamed the dream that most foster

18

children dream; the one of meeting my real parents. Yes, I know, when I met them everything would be ok. I would finally get the family that I wanted and deserved. I would have the love that I wanted but I didn't realize that God had another plan.

I have been going to church off and on since I was 15 years old. However, at the age of 23, I literally hit rock bottom. In January of 2004, I was trying to please everyone. I found myself trying to go to an event having only slept for a total of 4 hours after working an 18 hour shift prior. I was riding down the road as my car began to shake. I had noticed the shaking before but I had just got the car. In fact, I hadn't even made the first payment. How could this be? I was to make the first payment on January 5th and this was Saturday, January 3rd.

~The Wreck That Started My Road to Recovery~

After I got this car, I started noticing it shaking once I hit a certain speed. I was constantly running and kept saying I'll get it checked later but later never came. I was riding down the road and the car started shaking just a little and I didn't know if it was the car shaking or just the condition of the road that I was on. I kept driving and the next thing I knew the car started shaking uncontrollably and I couldn't gain control it. I looked around and remember saying "God, if you will save me from this, I'll stop playing church." That was the last thought that I had as my car hurled towards a light pole. I hit the light pole and I was knocked out. When I came through, I found myself dropped down in a ditch. The light pole was clearly cracked in half, there was dust everywhere and electrical lines lay all around me. I pulled myself together, open the door and walked across live wires to a nearby house. Everyone that came to help me said one thing, 'I don't know how you survived that.' I walked away with not one scratch and I knew it was only because of GOD.

It was from that point forward, that I started going to church. I made sure I was in church every Sunday, However, I was in church physically but my heart was still so clouded with hurt and pain. The word was coming forth but I wasn't allowing the Word to penetrate my heart the way it was supposed to. I was blinded by the hurt and the pain of my past and just sitting in church with my hands lifted up. Somehow, I knew that wasn't enough. The Lord knew that I needed a heart transplant and I didn't know where to start. I had gotten so far off track that I didn't even know the way to who I was. I had lost the identity in which God created for me. Somewhere under the stack of lies, it was there but I had lost my will to fight for my life, my purpose, and my destiny. We are all created for a purpose. Yet it seemed to me that my purpose was filled with hurt and pain. I was tired and it showed in everything that I did. I tried to fill the voids by doing stuff for people and then I would get mad and would say that people were using me when really, I was opening the door for them to use me. I never said no, even if it was giving my last little bit of money. I would do it in the hopes of being able to gain friendships, love, affection, and anything else in my opinion that my life was devoid of.

So often, we find ourselves at a point in our lives where we try to fill whatever we are missing with physical things. I thought I would finally get the love and affection that I wanted if I slept around, did stuff for people, or maybe if I was the tough one in the group. I had to be something to someone but one thing I couldn't be was myself. I didn't think anyone would care to be my friend if I they saw the real me. For years, I lived with rejection and the thought that if my real birth family didn't want me around, who would? The shame followed me like a dark cloud everywhere I went. Rejection, abandonment, fear, the feeling of worthlessness, shame, and abuse continued to follow me until I decided to break the chains that held me down.

You can say that you are tired. However, it is when you actually make up your mind to change that you will start overcoming your circumstances. I remember crying and screaming to the top of my lungs, banging on things, but nothing changed until it was a cry from my heart. A heart felt cry comes out of your mouth and your heart in order for you to actually start the process of being changed and healed. When you hold onto unnecessary things, you give sin legal grounds to invade your body, your finances, your family; you. That's why the Bible says, in your anger do not sin (Ephesian 4:26). This is a simple concept, which means that you should not to allow what is happening to you to get you to a point where it enrages you to react.

You see this happening on the news all the times where one moment of rage has changed a person's life forever. The number of murder and suicides has drastically increased where moments of rage have left many dead. Now, not only do they become victims of their emotions but they have also taken the lives of others and have left countless asking the question 'Why?" Your emotions are there to serve you but all too often, people allow their emotions to rule them. Even in my own life, I've seen where I have gotten angry and reacted out of my anger. Reacting as people in the world would act. You see it on TV, the streets, the news, and some see it in their own homes-Glorifying worldly things that we know are wrong. We see it so much that it's like second nature to react when someone does something to us. There are even parents who are teaching their own kids to react first and think later. I am not saying that we can't protect ourselves but protection and reacting are certainly two different things.

Young men are taught that crying is weak and that they have to be strong and the man of the house. Much of the imprisonment of young men and women could have been prevented if they thought before the reacted. When I talked to young men who have been or are currently in jail, many of them say that their moms told them that they needed to be the man of the house and that it was their responsibility to take care of the house. Did I miss something here? How can a 15 year old and some even younger, take on the responsibility of keeping a house? So, in a quest to prove their manhood, many of them turn to the wrong things to include selling drugs, stealing, and other acts of desperation to take care of a household that they aren't mature enough to handle.

This is not the way of God considering that we live in a society where God's voice is being shut out or muffled and the world's voice is becoming stronger with each passing day. We are allowing the things of this world to penetrate our hearts while unsavory thoughts and issues are becoming stronger and stronger each day. The bible says to:

> Keep thy heart with all diligence for out of it are the issues of life.
> (Proverbs 4:23, KJV emphasis added)

The heart has always been the place that holds our inner most thoughts; pain, hurt, etc. In the Message Bible, this same scripture reads as follows:

> Keep vigilant watch over your heart; that's where life starts
> (Proverbs 4:23, MSG, emphasis added)

When you keep a vigilant watch over something, you are constantly checking on it. You are watching it so carefully that the slightest little thing that is out of the ordinary, you jump on it immediately. Why can't we be like this after things come into our midst that doesn't line up with the word of God? We let things linger on for years that should have been dealt with immediately as soon as we recognize it. We should prance on it and rip it to pieces, but instead we let it stay and linger. We allow it to move in and it takes up legal grounds within us. Not only does it stay, it also brings unwanted houseguests with it.

When I was growing up, I was raped. This wasn't an ordinary rape, not that any rape is ordinary. But again, I say this wasn't ordinary because I was raped by a girl. Shortly after during a ride home on the bus, I was molested. The molestation was so physically painful. If I had to describe it I would have to say that having sex with a man was like going down on a kitchen chair with the wooden back that has two pointed ends. This thought had invaded my thoughts to the point that I can honestly say before going into a vow of abstinence, that I had never experienced intimacy. Emotions yes, but true intimacy, No. I wouldn't allow myself to trust a man to that point. This invasion of my mental and physical pain entered into my spiritual life to where I even found myself worshipping God with a wall up. How profoundly unfair?

I was seven when I was raped and eight when I was molested. For years, I thought these two incidents was what started it all; the drinking, partying, and having sex to feel affection. I felt like it had to start from there. But did it? Did I really have it mapped out correctly? Did I properly identify what started this chain of dreaded events in my life? Did I or would I have to dig deeper?

Chapter Five

Digging Deeper

As much as I wanted to stop right there, the answer was buried deep and I didn't want to go into the deep. When you're in the deep, you can't breathe as well as you can in shallow water. In the deep, you can't see the bottom. In the deep, you have to rely on your skills to keep you afloat. In the deep, there isn't any reference point to where you are; just water all around you. You may see something afar but how well can you see it? Is it crystal clear, can you make all the features out, or are you as many straining to see what you think you see?

I thought that my problems started when I was raped and molested, but in hindsight, I realize that they started long before that. Each of those unfortunate circumstances that happened to me, had a different effect on my life. It took something away from me but what gave it legal access to stay and to bring its friends? I was stuck at so many places all at once. I couldn't get over the rape. I couldn't get over the molestation. I couldn't get over other things in life. I would find myself repeating certain aspects over and over again.

It is always easier to deal with the surface issues instead of dealing with the real issues. It is always easier to blame God instead of dealing with the person(s) who really hurt you. I viewed it as since they didn't bother to acknowledge God, God quit bothering them and let them run loose. Then all hell broke loose, rampant evil. They made my life hell on earth with their envy, wanton, killing, bickering, and cheating. Look at them: mean spirited, venomous…. (Romans 1:28-32 MSG)

The King James Version says, "They were a reprobated minded people." They didn't have a mind to keep good so He gave them over to a reprobated mind. It is easy for us to blame God and to say "Why did God allow this to happen to me?"

Conversely, we don't want to admit that God has given all of us choices and it is up to us to decide which way to turn. Some of us will make good decisions while others will make not-so-good choices.

When hurting, often times we forget that God has given us all choices. We blame God and point the finger at Him instead of saying that this person is the reason that I got hurt. In order to deal with what is going on with you, you have to acknowledge that you are hurting. We walk through life with the "I'm OK Syndrome," knowing good and well that we aren't ok at all. We are hurting and want to be free. Things such as pride, unforgiveness, or self-promise holds us back from living the life that God intended for us to live. He wants us to live the good life. He wants us to be free. Life is full of ups and downs. Too often we get stuck in the downs. He never said that life will be pain free and hurt free. He did promise us that we will have a Comforter to be with us throughout the journey.

I thank God for the Holy Spirit and His ability to comfort me. We walk around like trained zombies, trying to fool ourselves with work! You know the ones that when the church doors open, they are always there. You know…the faithful ones. The ones that know the scripture says 'Work alone will not get you in Heaven.' It is easier to trick the public than to be real with yourself. To show any kind of weakness is not an option. That person quotes scriptures in their heads to justify the work that they do in the church and then when scriptures doesn't work, they go to the self-promise if I don't do it then who will?

Yep. This was me. I know all aspects of the church from running the media, to even doing the bookkeeping. I never did the book keeping at Zion Hopewell Full Gospel Family Worship Center but I have had the privilege of doing it at another church. I knew how to do it all and there was no stopping me. Even when I tried to pull away, many people wouldn't allow me to. So, the self-promises started to build up. I got to the point where I started hating the church. I remember going home one Wednesday night crying and feeling underappreciated, full and most of all, burned out. While crying, I started talking to God and telling Him how I was feeling and I heard nothing. Finally I said, God, I don't know what to do. I don't even know why I am feeling this way. Finally He answered and said "You are feeling underappreciated because of the obligation, not because of what I have asked you to do." When I heard that, I realize that I was feeling this way not because of the burden He had given me but because of the burden that I had allowed myself and others to put on me.

After I realized this, I ask God to tell me how to correct it all so I could stop hating church. He didn't answer me until later. In my bathroom getting ready for bed and; I was standing there looking in the mirror when I heard him say "You can't hate what I created." Looking deep in the mirror, I pondered what He said. I knew that I was the church, but I wasn't talking about hating myself I was talking about hating the physical church. I was thinking, 'OK God, you have missed it this time,' and before I could even speak it, He said "No I haven't. You hate the physical church because you are using it as a cover up. You are trying not to face what you know it is time to face. Instead of facing it, you find more and more to do in the church." I got defensive. 'No, I am not. I didn't ask to do some of this stuff, I was volunteered to do it.' He said, "That may be the case but why didn't you say no?" Good question, why didn't I say no. I mean aren't you supposed to be working in the church? No unemployment in the church. The church is where you are supposed to develop a good character of integrity. You don't want to displease anyone. So you try to help out. Isn't that the Christian thing to do? Then He hit me with the ultimate "The Christian thing to do is to please me." Silence and nothing else followed.

I continued to stare in the mirror and then tears started to flow. I hated the person that I was becoming. I was at a brick wall and felt like there was nowhere else to go. Even though I felt like my back was against the brick wall, I felt as if there was a continual beating going on. I felt so heavy and tired, that I didn't know where else to go. Every day I got up and I felt like I was taking my body and slamming it up against a brick wall. Why wouldn't the brick wall break? I am hitting it as hard as I can! I'm doing all that I know how to do but why won't it come down? I prophesied to others and helped them break free of their chains but where was the prophecy for me? Why can't someone prophesy to me about how to get this brick wall down? Where are the saints who were supposed to be praying for me? Did they come down off the wall because I felt like I was living in HELL. The heat was up and I was tired, drained, and felt like giving up. Where were the angels that would come to renew my strength? I was standing there alone looking in the mirror as tears streamed down my face. I started crying out, "Lord I just want to be FREE! Free from my past, free from my mind, just free." Then He spoke, "The doors are open why aren't you walking out of it?" I answered, "Because I am afraid of what is on the other end and what will happen if I finally closed the door." I had identified so much with my past, that it was now a part of me. Who was I if I didn't have my past to justify my nasty attitude? Who was I if I didn't have my past to justify my behavior? Who was I?

I was nothing..........I continued to cry and headed towards my bedroom. When finally, He spoke again, "You will be free to be the one I've created you to be." But who is that? I had spent my entire life playing the chameleon that I had forgotten who I was. No longer could I continue to play this game and be true to God. As much as I loved people, I loved God more and I had a hunger, and a thirst to please Him. He wants me to be free and I wanted to be free but I knew the road to freedom was going to be a hard one.

For so long, I had used the church as a cover up. Growing up in the foster care system, I felt as though I was neglected by my family. Yes, I have a foster family and I am thankful for them but I still had a feeling of loneliness. I stood off feeling lonely and thinking no one cared for or loved me. So, when I found a

27

great church home in Zion Hopewell Full Gospel Family Worship Center, I was like, "Yes, this is it!" So, to get what I thought I wanted, I started doing as much as I could in the church. I had a need to be needed. If I couldn't help, I felt as though I was worthless so I worked and worked. I hardly ever missed church. Then, something started to change. I stopped wanting to go to church to get the feel of family. I started wanting my own. I wanted the feeling of family to continue without having to run to the church every time the church doors opened. I wanted my own and I could no longer hide behind doing work in the church to camouflage it.

Making up your mind to be free is the hardest thing to do. Once your mind is made up and you are no longer fighting the battle in your mind, you've won 75 percent of the battle. Now, comes the hard part. You have to face the demons of your past and take the authority away that you've gave them and finally run into your freedom. Are you ready to run free?

Therefore if any man be in Christ, he is a new creature; the old things are passed away; behold, all things are become new.

II Corinthians 5:17

Chapter Six

Wheelchair Syndrome

Everyone has a wheelchair that they have to get out of. It isn't a physical wheelchair but a mental one. Something has happened that for some reason, seems to keep us trapped. For me, I was trapped in the negative mindset of failure; that no one will ever love me and I was a nobody. By rolling those thoughts around in my head every day, I became immobilized. If you keep stopping at the place where you have been hurt, will constantly find yourself going back to that point and reliving it. We have put that person in a wheelchair and mentally they roll with us everywhere we go. You may hear people say that you need to let that little girl or boy inside of you go. They aren't talking about your youthfulness but the idea that you have someone trapped inside of you that is causing you to be bitter. Someone who has been hurt so bad that until you let that person go, that part of your life will remain immobile.

I was given up for adoption and even though my family didn't tell me that I was adopted immediately. I sensed that I didn't belong. I remember spending countless hours and days outside or somewhere by myself. It wasn't until I was eight years old and out of a fit of anger, that my mother told me that I was adopted. It was at that point that I felt like everything changed. I started feeling even more displaced and like no one wanted me. In my eyes, if the ones who had taken their time to create me didn't want me, then who would? I fought with realizing my self-worth for years. As the years went on, more weight was added until I was paralyzed. I was so paralyze with the world's view of myself, that I could not see God's view. Many times in life, we find ourselves weighted down with things that have happened to us in the past. We cannot rightfully obtain what God has promised us because we are weighed down with what went wrong, the 'what ifs' of our lives. God never meant for us to get caught up in the world.

We are in this world but not of this world. John 17:16 KJV

This scripture reminds us that even though we live in this world, we are not of this world. There are scriptures after scriptures that tell us of the promises of God. However, we don't pick up the word of

God, and allow it to enter our spirit to push us forward as much as we allow the world to enter into our spirit which holds us in bondage. From the TV, to family, to the radio, to what we say about ourselves, we allow all kinds of things to speak to us. We allow what is said, to be dominating in our lives instead of the Word of God. It is very important that we renew our mind daily. Studying and meditating on the Word of God assists us with deflecting those things that the world says about us. If you don't, you will find yourself constantly doubting yourself and feeling insecure. The world is constantly changing; one minute being skinny is in, then the next, it isn't. As the world changes, so will its view of you. The same breath that accepted you, can also reject you, leaving you hopeless and empty.

Predators are constantly on the lookout for people that they can control. They look for those who have low self-esteem because they know that they will be easy to manipulate and use them at their advantage. People who rape and molest people are those types of predators. They go after those who they do not feel will fight back and will just go with the flow of what they are doing. This is why it is important to know who you are in God. When you know who you are in God, it will bring forth a confidence and boldness that you can't explain. When you are confident, you will not just go along with anything and everything. You will know your self-worth and won't allow anything that doesn't enhance you to stay.

~The Beginning of My Wall~

I was raped and molested but the molestation was far worse than the rape. I was riding home on the bus, sitting alone as I did many days. I remember wearing a brown skirt and a yellow turtle neck; a target for bullying. So like most days, the bus was filled to capacity and one of the high school students would have to sit with me. I sat on the seat, looking out of the window day-dreaming, when a familiar high school student sat on the seat with me. He had sat on the seat next to me before, so I was familiar him. But this day was different. He sat so close to me that he trapped my right arm against his body. He draped his left arm around me and pulled me close to him. He made a hug-like gesture and pinned my left arm with his forearm. Immediately, I remembered fear building up inside of me. I tried to tell him that he was squeezing me and then he started to feel on me. Tears started to flow and one of the girls on the bus turned around and asked why I was crying because no one said anything to me. Fearing I was about to say something, he started picking at me. I remember his exact words as he said it three times in a row. He started to grope me. He continued to laugh and pick at me and others on the bus joined in with him. When I started crying louder, he bent me over and started fondling me. He kept doing it until the bus came to my stop. I was the first stop, so as the bus rounded the corner, he straightens up and looked at me. He smiled and said 'now go on with your ugly self.' As I passed him, he patted me on my bottom and started laughing.

I got off that bus feeling used and abused. I ran up the steps past my momma and daddy who were working on something in the yard. My daddy saw me crying and he assumed that I crying because the other kids had been picking at me. But as I rushed passed them, I heard my mother say "no this is something different." She came into my room asking me what happened; I couldn't stop crying long enough to say anything but I mimicked the hand motions. I didn't know his name but I remember seeing him in one of my siblings' year books. I found him, pointed him out and I never saw him on the bus again. I thought that was the end of my dilemma but unfortunately, it was only the beginning. I would run into him again years later and to my horror, he remembered me but I didn't remember him. My mind had mentally blocked out his face but I remembered every time I saw him I would become fearful. One day he made the mistake of saying I was that same little bitch that was on that bus. It was at this point that I remembered who he was. I remember feeling afraid all over again.

I became that little girl on the bus all over again but this time I vowed that he wouldn't hurt me like that again. I would be the strong one and he wouldn't hurt me again. I started building up my defense and was determined that he would never be able to hurt me like he did in times past. When you've been hurt to this magnitude, you make up inner vows. These inner vows are a form of protection most of the time. They are vows you make to help protect yourself from the hurt and the abuse that you once felt. I made up this inner vow and I thought I would always be able to protect myself from him hurting me again, but I was wrong.

I went to visit a friend who had asked me to come over. As I knocked on the door and the door opened, he was on the other side. Fear immediately overwhelmed me. I walked through the open door and he closed it behind me. I immediately called out for my friend and he said, "Oooh she went to the store and will be back, go ahead and have a seat." He stood in front of the door and wouldn't move until I sat down on the couch. Once I sat down, he moved to the kitchen table where he could look directly at me. He then started complimenting me. I wouldn't answer him. I stayed for about ten minutes as he continued to make vulgar comments about me and my looks. He got up from where he was sitting to go into one of the back room. Saying that he was going to get his phone and take a picture of me. I saw this as my opportunity to escape. I stood up and said, "Tell her I will see her later" and ran to the door. He ran behind me, grabbed my

34

arm and pulled me to him once again, trapping me. All I could say was, "God please, not again." I started crying and telling him to let me go. He kept saying 'no I got to take this picture of you for tonight.' We fought and fought. I knew I needed to get out of the door. The more I struggled to get to the door, the stronger he became. I struggled and fought with him trying to get to the door and he would pull me back. The door was my only hope. It was raining that night so I knew no one would be out walking. Once again, I felt hopeless and alone. I thought to myself, "If I can get to the door and get it open, he would stop because he didn't want to take the chance of getting caught." So I fought.

He was so much stronger then I was. I just kept saying, 'Jesus please help me,' 'Jesus please help me.' I kept fighting and trying to get out of the door but he kept trying to pull me back in. Finally, I got one of my arms loose and I hit him hard enough that he let me go. I got to the door, opened it and ran out of the apartment, but he was on my trail. He caught me again at the steps of the apartment. It was raining so my skin was wet and his grip wasn't as good and I was able to slip out of his grasp and ran to my car. He stood at the bottom of those steps laughing at me as I drove off. I remembered getting to my apartment and sitting in my car and crying. I let it happen again. I called myself all kinds of names. I was so mad at myself. I was supposed to protect myself from him. How could I allow him to do that again? You are a grown woman. I gave myself the beat down.

After that I became fearful all over again. Once again I had become the little girl. I had to protect myself. I started hiding and walking in a spirit of shame because in my eyes I had failed myself. I had FAILED and I beat myself up about that for years. I remembered being so ashamed, that I never told anyone until recently, while doing volunteer work and speaking to a group about being sexually abused. I let my molester take my peace from me because I never told anyone what happened. I became so fearful of him and ashamed, that this situation had happened again. That demon felt like he had the right to do whatever he wanted to do to me because I wouldn't say anything.

From that point, he made it a constant decision that whenever he saw me he would intimidate me every chance he got. He even had the nerve to get a job near where I lived. I didn't know until one day when I went grocery shopping and I saw him. I turned around going down another aisle and he continued to follow me. He followed me while I shopped. Then, he would go outside when I put my groceries in the car and watch me drive away. I put myself in a self-made prison. I stopped going to that store. I stopped going any place that I thought I would see him. In my head, this was the only way. I thought I could just ignore it away but I couldn't.

I had to nullify the legal ground that this spirit felt he had the right to do whatever he wanted to me. I didn't understand why he kept trying to hurt me. I was eight years old when he molested me and thirty when he attacked me. I started praying and as I continue to pray, I realized that the molestation had caused a soul tie with him. A soul tie is a tie that connects two people together. It causes a bond between the two people. I had to break the soul tie first in order to be free from him. I started cancelling the soul tie between me and him by first forgiving him. Once I forgave him, it broke up the legal ground for that spirit to rule in. Then, I started working on how the molestation and the attack had hurt me. This process was hard for me because I was constantly running into him. Every time I saw him, I would become that hurt little girl again; fearful and shameful all over again. He would laugh at me and I would walk away. Finally, a breakthrough happened and the shame of the molestation and the attack no longer held me bound. It came during one of the inner healing classes at my church. I had to change the locks and the only way to change the locks was to do a clean sweep of my own life from him, evict him and then get the MASTER LOCKSMITH to come in and change all the locks. Once the locks were changed, I was no longer ashamed to share my

36

testimony of how I was molested and attacked by him. The process it took to get free from this situation was a tough one. Many times, I attempted to just sweep it under the rug and pretend like it never happened. I would run into him and the fear would rise back up. That fear was a constant reminder that I hadn't dealt with that situation. That I couldn't keep escaping into that place in my mind where nothing ever happened when it did. I needed to be set free but was I willing to go through the process to become free?

The righteous cry, and the Lord
heareth, and delivereth them out of all of
their troubles. The Lord is nigh unto
them that are of a broken heart; and
saveth such as be of a contrite spirit.
Many are the afflictions of the righteous:
but the Lord delivereth him out of them
all. He keepeth all his bones: not one of
them is broken.

Psalm 34: 17-20 KJV

Chapter Seven

The Spirit of Rejection

The spirit of rejection is a huge strong man that has a lot of little leeches that comes with it. Every one of the things that I spoke of previously was leeches from the spirit of rejection. I was given up for adoption at an early age. Even though the first home that I went to, I ended up being adopted, I always thought that I did not fit in. Some people say that there was no reason for me to feel like that. I remember at the age of seven, I would walk around feeling alone even though I was in a crowded room. I could never understand why until I took the inner healing class at my.

It was in these classes that we analyzed things that have hindered us and started attacking the main spirit. I could not understand why I could get prayed for depression and it leaves me at that moment but later it would come back. I will never forget the first time that I heard my Pastor's voice which I felt was aimed directly towards me. We were in our annual women's conference and the speaker of the night was Apostle Deborah Chiles. The enemy was attacking her body and my pastor said that we need some women who know how to pray to under gird this woman and let the enemy know we are not going to stand for it. Well I was not scared to pray. So I went up and I began to pray with the other women for the healing of her body. All of a sudden, I started fighting and I heard my pastor's voice as clear as day say, "You fighting Depression". He was right. I was fighting a serious case of depression because I was contemplating suicide. I had gotten back to that point in my life. Well those feelings were broken on that day but it came back a couple of months later and I could not understand why. It was because I had not dealt with the strong man. The Spirit of Rejection.

I am using a term called strong man that you may not be familiar with. A strong man is something that has a heavy

39

presence in your life that can cause you to make life-changing decisions but in the wrong spirit. Whether it is out of fear or anxiety, you will find yourself making hasty decisions. The strong man can make you feel inadequate and like you would never measure up. The best way to can explain the differences between a strong man and a symptom of a strong man is this:

Imagine that you have a big strong tree. Now, this tree has branches, roots, and a trunk. Now, the strong man is the roots. Without the roots of a tree, the tree cannot live. If you only attack the branch, after a while, the branch will grow back. Then, you have some that are stronger than the others. The stronger one in this example would be the trunk of the tree, because you can cause damage to the trunk but it does not take the tree down. You have to attack the root.

Let me explain it like this: the root of the problem was the 'Spirit of Rejection' the branches were the sickness, headaches, arthritis, ulcers, and migraines. The trunk was alcoholism, depression, and suicide. This was the tree. When we had healing services at my church and they called out a symptom that I was having I would jump up and get prayed for, feel great but just like you cut a branch off of a tree, you still leave a stub of the branch letting someone know that a branch was once there. I would be all right for a little while and then I would end up getting sick again. Then, it was my trunk; the battle with alcoholism, depression, and suicide. They were what I turned to when things were not going right, especially alcoholism. I could kick that tree trunk and let it know that I had been there with a powerful kick but it was still standing. I did not do enough damage to kill the tree. Then there was my root, the 'Spirit of Rejection.' It was not until I dealt with this that was I finally able to win the battle over these problems.

The Spirit of Rejection was my strong man. You have to take the time to identify what is yours. I was in church praising God, following behind my pastors, being an active member in the church, but I felt no change. I felt like the only reason that I was going to church was because that was what was expected of me and it fed my longing to have a family. I could not understand why I was not seeing the fruit. I was physically, emotional, and spiritual torn. I was trying so hard but it was as though I could not see the change. It was not until I learned how to cast that Spirit of Rejection down, that I began to know who I was and whose I was. It was not until I came into the Agape love of God and know that it was during those times in which I thought that I walked alone that He was truly there because of His connection with me. It was when I realized that before I was saved and even came into his presence that His hand of grace and mercy was still covering me, He was just waiting on me to look up to Him. He was waiting on me.   When I think that He was waiting on me, my heart becomes full. For so long, I was looking for man to do it when God had already done it. He made me whole.

When I identified the strong man in my life and start coming against that area the branches started coming down. I started coming against all of the sickness that was trying to attach itself to my body. I immediately started coming against that spirit of alcoholism, but it was not until I identified my strong man that I was able to do that. It was not until I stop giving the devil so much credit and started looking in the mirror and realizing that I was my own worst enemy and that I had given the enemy too much credit for self-inflicted wounds. The enemy might have opened the door but it is our choice whether or not we keep that door open.

In my case with the Spirit of Rejection, I have to continually come against that spirit. Every time a thought comes in that does not line itself up with the word of God, I have to immediately cast it down because everything that we do starts with a thought. It is left up to you to decide what thoughts will rule you today and what thoughts you will cast down. This is when you learn how to deal with yourself and stop saying and giving the glory to Satan. You have to remember he was thrown out of heaven because he thought himself above God. So, he loves it when you give him glory for something that he has not done. I've sometimes heard it said that the enemy is crying because we are blaming him for things he doesn't do. I don't agree with that statement. If Satan and a host of rebellious angels were thrown out of heaven because they thought to exalt him over God, in my opinion he would be sitting back saying, "Yeah give me some more glory, hit me again, and exalt my name over the one who you say have your back." Oh I love it when you praise my name. This is my thought, 'if I am not putting all of my focus and attention on God and on something else, then I am exalting that thing.' Let it be negative or positive, I am still giving that thing my attention. However, when a situation comes up, instead of focusing my attention on that, I just stand up and give God the praise. Then guess what? I have redirected my attention from the situation and put it back on God for He is the one who deserves the glory. Matthew 6:36, "Seek ye first the Kingdom of God and all these things shall be added to you," So if I seek and praise the Kingdom of God instead of sitting there and worrying over a situation; then God will handle it. Well guess what? 'Glory be to God, Glory to your name' is what I am going to be saying.

I don't want to give the enemy any attention. I want him to know that he is under my feet. I love God and I want him to show himself strong in me and the only way I know how to do that is to glorify his name. You see too many people walking around with a smile on the outside but hurting on the inside. God doesn't want your happiness to be something that the people see. He wants it to be where the people know you are genuinely happy. He wants to know that your smile is a direct reflection of what is going on in the inside of you because He wants to be abundantly free.

How many *are* mine iniquities and sins? make me to know my transgression and my sin.

Job 13:23

Chapter Eight

Dealing with Yourself

For a long time, I thought I had it all together. I thought I had everything that I needed. I didn't trust anyone beyond what I could see and I would often tell people I was a hard-hitting woman who didn't need a man but for one thing. I didn't need anyone and I kept my hurt covered. Through the years of being mistreated, I learned how to cover my heart, from trust, love, and family. I had a covering over my heart that wouldn't allow me see beyond those boundaries.

I made it tough for anyone to love me. My thought process was, if you really loved me you would see beyond what I was saying and see how my heart was hurting. Many people tried but not many succeeded. I had my own cheering section in my head and every time someone didn't do something that I wanted them to do or didn't acknowledge me, 'the voice,' would go off in my head saying, "I told you so. They didn't mean you any good. Why did you trust them? They are just like everyone else." The conversation would continue until my heart would harden against that person. I was building a stony heart against that person so when they came around again, they would regret ever coming. I would sit there and devise a plan that I knew would hurt them. I was cut throat and didn't want to be the only one on the other side of the fence of hurt. I didn't care how small it was. It could have been something as simple as; I would text someone and they would not answer me. The voice would pop-up....." You are bothering them. They didn't mean what they said. They don't care about you." I couldn't understand why that voice had so much power, how it could make me change my attitude and be totally mean to a person who cared about me. I had only one person to blame this voice on and that was the Devil. It had to be the Devil. It couldn't be me. Or could it?

In all honesty, it wasn't the Devil. One day, I flipped on someone who I cared about a lot. This person has never done anything but shown me love and as much as I could not understand why they were there, I also couldn't not understand them not being there. Part of me wanted that person to go ahead and hurt me so that I could be right. I knew it was coming sooner or later.

This was the hardest part for me, saying it wasn't my fault. I was plagued by so much guilt. I had become this self-independent, angry woman who thought she did not need anyone or anything. I was raped and even though I was, I still went through the process but I could never really engage in it. The rape had put up a mental block in my mind and even though I went through the process, I could not fully trust the person that I was with. Mentally, I could not go there but physically I did. Most people have sex because physically, you can have sex but there are very few that make love. Making love is a more of a mental thing rather just a physical. By not dealing with the pain, you give yourself a false truth. Just because you have the ability to do something doesn't mean that you have dealt with the situation. You are walking around with invisible bags on and each one has a trigger that can set you off. When you don't deal with the situation that caused you hurt, it becomes an infected wound that will start affecting you in more than one way by not properly tending to it.

You have to deal with the things that would be so easy to forget. Although you cannot excuse your rapist or your molester, or the person who hurt you, let me be the first one to tell you, "It was not your fault and you did nothing. I mean nothing to deserve having something so precious taken away." For years, I literally hated myself. I could not stand to look at myself in the mirror. I could not stand to be left in a room and hear myself because I was scared of hearing anything that I had to say because I did not think that I was worthy enough to speak into my own life. I had such a low self-esteem issue, that a couple of years ago was my

45

first time looking in the mirror and saying that I was beautiful. I would walk around with my head down scared to look people in the eye. People would say to me, 'Stop walking with your head down. You can't see where you are going.' Even though that was true, part of me didn't care where I was going because in my mind I was not worthy enough to go anywhere.

It was years of believing that it was my fault that brought on everything that had happened to me. Because of what happened to me, sex was the only way to get someone of the opposite sex to want me. I'm not ashamed to say it but for the longest time I never even taught about getting married. My aim was to have a live-in boyfriend. I thought that as long as I got a live-in boyfriend, that was all that I needed. I didn't need anything else because I was not going to be able to get anything else. That is what years of believing that type of thinking it was your fault will do for you. It'll make you think that you are not worthy of anything and that you better accept what you have because that is the best that you can get. Well, I am here to tell you, "The Devil is a liar." It is God's intention for us to have the best of everything; he said in his word in

Genesis 1:26
"Let us create man in our image,"

Psalms 139:14
"You are fearfully and wonderfully made,"

Deuteronomy 28:13
"You are the head and not the tail, above and not beneath."

When I was in the world no one came and told me these things. They came and told me "You are ugly, you too fat, your lips are not big enough, or your teeth are too big. Then, we go and get in the church with this same mindset; unwilling to change (I know because I have done it) because we have let the world identify us. My pastor, Apostle Theotis White made a powerful statement one morning in Morning Glory (you may call it Sunday school). He said we are ready to accept the world's view and ready to reject God's word. When he said that, it rung in my ears because God's word is true. He said that in Matthew 24:35, "Heaven and earth will pass away, but My words will by no means pass away." I know that we are living in the last days. I have heard enough messages to know. The last time I checked, I was still standing on earth, heaven is still above me. If I am doing all of that, then guess what, God's word is still reigning true.

We have to break out of the mindset of the world. The world has put us in a box. If you don't weigh this, then you are too fat. If you don't look like this, then you are ugly. Well God created me and when he did he said in Genesis 1:31, "It was very good." Every time God created something in Genesis 1 he stated "it was good." He created me. So therefore, I am good. If I am good then, that's all that matters.

God gave you the power to walk over scorpions and not be harmed. He also gave you the power to cast down any vain imagination that will exalt itself over him. In other words... YOU ARE OWN YOUR WORST ENEMY!! Nothing has power over you unless you give it the right to have dominion over you. Once something dominates you, you start seeing changes in your decision making process and even in your daily walk because you allowed a thought to enter into your mind. A thought that is contrary to the Will of God. The Bible says to renew your mind daily. That means you have to keep constantly refreshing your mind to defeat those thoughts that aren't in alignment with the Will of God.

When you start standing in the power that God has given you and stop allowing yourself to be someone's garbage can, worldly things can no longer dominate you. A garbage can holds unwanted items; things we no longer have a use for. When you allow someone to put things in your spirit that are not in

47

alignment with what God has already said about you, then you are being someone's garbage can. We have to stop allowing people to put their point of views in our head. God's word is true and is not going to say that you are fearfully and wonderfully made and then turn around and say, "You're ugly" or "You're Fat." That is not the God I serve.

I'm not saying that it's okay to be so big that it is unhealthy. The Bible states Jesus "came so that you can have life and have it more abundantly" (John 10:10). You cannot have that if you are unhealthy to the point where you can't enjoy life. For the longest, we as a people, especially women, have become accustomed to saying what we don't have or what we are lacking. When we begin to embrace ourselves and start seeing ourselves as the beautiful creature that God has created; then those negative mind sets will have no room to stand.

When I was dealing with the 'Spirit of Rejection,' I found that I had misinterpreted being needed for being loved. I thought that if I made myself indispensable to people, they would need me and love me. That was not the case.

Love has no attachments. You do not have to do anything to receive it. Love is freely given to you. In the Word of God it states that 'you owe no man but to love them." At one point in my life, I was literally trying to please everyone with either buying or working for their love. I thought that I had to work for their love. I thought that I had to earn their love because that was all I knew how. I was out trying to please everyone else forgetting the main reason that I was created; to please God.

I was so busy trying to be everyone's superwoman. I could not say 'no' to anyone because I thought that I would lose out on something. I couldn't take time out for myself if someone else was calling on me to do something because I thought that was selfish. All of my life, I've associated love with the concept of being needed. If I wasn't needed, then I was not loved. That was my way of thinking. After the wreck that nearly cost me my life, I still could not see what I was doing. I didn't catch it until my Pastor, Apostle Theotis White, taught a Wednesday night service about "Dealing with Your Stress." Through his teaching, I was able to identify so many things that I was doing that added undue stress on my body. My friends would call me while I was at home when I just wanted to take some time for myself. They would say come over. I'm bored. In my mind, I am thinking that I am a Christian and I was supposed to help meet the needs of the people because sometimes we are the only Bible that they will read. I had to get up and go. I had to make time in my schedule even though I was already stressing; knowing that I would get the blessing in the end. That is not in the word of God. I had to realize one thing that God says "you go when I send you and when you do, you go in my strength. There I was again; confusing love with being needed.

Love has no attachment. Love comes freely and just as it comes freely; you can receive it freely. You do not have to do anything to receive it except be the best you that you can be. When mothers have babies, those babies do nothing for the love that is poured on them. They just sit back and receive it. One day God asked me how open was I to receiving what he has for me. I thought that is a crazy question. I said you hear my decree. I want all that you have for me. He said, "no you don't because what I give to you, you reject it." For so long, I was used to love with conditions. If you don't do this, then I am mad at you or don't want you around. I had to get off that track and learn how to live in the moment and know that God's love has no attachments.

I am learning how to do this. It's not just something that you are going to wake up the next day and say 'I am going to trust this person.' If you have been hurt multiple times, especially if it has been from the people whom you believed were supposed to support you, it is going to be a step by step process. I was 26 and I was raped and molested by the age of 9. I had serious issues

49

when it came to closeness with people and at the age of 25. I learned how to give a hug without second guessing it. Did it take 17 years? No, it did not take that long, once I learned how to take down my strong man. The trust came for those people who I knew meant me good. I am not saying that it will not be a one-day process. You have to first heal from the hurt. Then you have to learn how to love yourself. If you love you, you will not let anything happen to you. When you are able to love yourself; you will have that same protection and won't let just anyone come around you and put you down, or cause you hurt or harm. You will not allow anything to come to you that is not decent and in order.

I believe the reason so many young people who are having babies and letting men do any and everything to them is because they have not learned how to love and accept themselves. How do I know? I used to be there. I had no respect for myself. I believed that I didn't deserve the best so I had to work to keep what I had. It was better to have something then to have nothing. I thought that I had to work for love and acceptance, when all I had to do was to accept it.

Take this short quiz

1. Do you love yourself?

2. When was the last time you accepted a gift from someone without thinking that they wanted something in return?

3. After reading this chapter, do you see where your goal was to please people and not God?

4. In the last three months, have you put your plans to do something on the back burner to do something for someone else? If so how many times?

This quiz was designed just to make you aware of yourself. Sometimes, we can do something out of habit and not realize that it was not a good habit. It is not good for you to take so much time trying to please everyone and put yourself last. You have to take time for yourself. This will help you build yourself up and help you to develop in other areas of your life.

Chapter Nine

Accepting the Past as the Past and Moving On

For twenty-five years, I was a bag lady. I carried around on so much baggage from my past. I had it all in my head, believed it and lived it every day. What happened to me in my past, left me scared, but guess what, just like any scar, I healed. I just needed the right remedy in order to heal. In the physical realm, when you break your skin, it starts to bleed, which is usually the first sign that you've been hurt. After realizing that you are bleeding, you go and rinse off the area so that you can gain a better view to see if this is something you can deal with or will you need to go to the doctor. It's the same process when you are hurting internally as well.

You have to first realize that you are hurting. Once you realize the hurt, it's time to analyze what is causing you to feel that way. There are some things that you will have to deal with on your own, because it will be up to you to decide what you are willing to do to get over "it". For example, in the middle of 2007, I fought through a tough battle of alcoholism. Did I drink? No. One day I was drinking water and all of a sudden I could taste the liquor in my mouth as if had I just swallowed it. That was me showing myself that I did not have to turn to liquor to make me feel better. All I had to do was look unto the hill from which comes my help but I also had to go through the process of being delivered from it so that it would not have a strong hold on me.

Like any injury, you cannot leave a cut unattended. You have to make sure that it stays clean and free of infection. Okay let's stop. When you are being healed you have to make sure you are in the right environment. You have to surround yourself with people who can see where you are going, so when your feet get weak they will help you stand strong. In life, I've found that there are two types of friends in which I will reference the scripture to explain both of them. In the book of Matthew, there are two cripple people; one sat at the gates of Beautiful and the other was brought in through the roof. The one who sat at the gates of Beautiful, his friends brought him there every day. Friends that will help you stay in your mess and not help you out of it. They are the ones who will not be able to see you beyond where you are currently. These are be the ones chanting in your ear 'that's good, you better stay right there' (in all of your mess).

Then you have the ones that will be like the friends who took the roof off and let their friend in because they saw his future and they were not going to let it slip past them. They are the ones who will say "you can get better," "you can do better," "you just have to believe in yourself." Those are the ones who you need to keep around you, because they are the ones who will help push you into your future when you don't want to go. You have to make the decision about what type of friends you want around you. If you have friends who will help you stay in your mess, you need to do some rearranging. If you have friends who will tear the roof down to make sure you get to your blessing, you better keep them close to you. They will be your own personal army forging the way so that you can go through. They will be the ones that will be praying for you when you don't even want to pray for yourself.

After you have cleaned your cut and it has healed, the cut will heal in time. You may be left with a scar to indicate that there was a cut there but it will be healed. Let's stop here. Once your cut has been healed you may have a scar but it is not for you to linger on. It is for the next person. I have this saying, 'First I am tested and while I am being tested I may moan 'Why' but afterwards, I have a testimony.' You see, once you are healed you have now been put in a position where you can help someone else. You are able to go out and help someone else who has been hurt by something that you

53

may have been through. The difference is... you made it! You have to make that decision and God will lead you to let you know when it is time for you to share your testimony. You have to use wisdom because even though you may have the best intentions; everyone cannot handle your nakedness. For me, I am an open person and there are some things in which God has not allowed me to share. I have recently just started talking about my rape and molestation publicly. As I said earlier, this was something that I was highly ashamed of. I was not at a point where I could help someone else because I had not been healed. I had to accept the past and move on. As long as I was letting the past rule me, I was letting God know that I did not believe in him. I could not trust God to the point where I could lay all of my burdens to him. This was hard for me to finally accept, but through the help of good friends, whom God placed in my life, I was able to conqueror that fear and many more. I was so scared of what people would think, how they would view me and that I was not pleasing God but myself.

Take the time to answer these short questions:

1. Is there a past hurt that you still remember vividly?

2. If so, what is causing this memory to be so painful?

3. Have you decided that you want to forgive this person?

4. Have you forgiven everyone that was associated with that situation?

5. Are you at a point where you can talk about your situation?

There are situations that I still have a hard time talking about; because they are still very raw and emotional for me. If God puts it on my heart to share it; I will trust Him enough to do so. He will always direct you. He won't leave you uncovered and protect you. That is the one thing I have learned the most about Him. His goal is to keep you covered. He will never leave you nor forsake you. So even in those moments where you are trying to break free and you find yourself saying, "No, I can't say anything because people will look at me" that's the enemy trying to let the spirit of shame conquer you. Surely you must know that God is bigger than anything that is against you and His love has the ability to conqueror ALL. Not some, but ALL things!

Chapter 10

Stick with the Plan

There are people out there who have been living in situations and have not dealt with their issues. Instead, they have been masking it up with other things. My point is that it is time to stop using temporary fixes for what seems like a life-long problem. I can never change the fact that I was raped or molested but I can change how it affects my future life. It is up to you to decide how you will ultimately attack your situation.

As I mentioned, I have been through a lot but my plan of attack had to be altered for each situation. I cannot approach Problem A, the same way I approach Problem B. There may be some similarities but the plans have to be different. Once I found an attack that worked, I stuck with it. That's the key, you have to get your plan of attack and stick with it. You have to approach this with the same mindset as though you are trying to lose weight. If your goal is to do something you stick with it. That same principles that you apply in the natural world, have to be applied within your spiritual world. This is spiritual warfare.

You have to find your plan and stick with it. Spiritual warfare is not something to play with. The enemy can approach with the same thing that you thought that you were over. If you have your attack plan in order, you will know exactly what to do. If you don't have a plan, this blow can take you back to square one.

Let me explain something. In this book, I have informed you of how I dealt with a serious case of rejection and the moment I thought that I was over it, guess what, I was forced to deal with rejection again. All of my life I thought that I was given up for adoption at birth only to find out that was not true. One day I went to visit my grandfather and we were talking, I made mention of the adoption and he said no. I said what, he said no again. The "no" did not register and I was like "what are you talking about."

56

He told me a story that was different from what I had been told my entire life. That day I went home and cried and the Spirit of Rejection started coming back stronger and stronger until I remembered I had a plan. When my plan of attack formed in my mind and I started attacking that spirit by boldly saying, "This has no control over me." I can't control how I ended up here on this earth. All I can control it, how I let each day affect me or how I affect it.

Without my plan of attack, I would have done just that; went and got in my bed right back at square one. You have to make the decision to leave it all behind and conquer whatever it is. You have to make that a goal within yourself.

Step One-   Admit that there is a problem.

Step Two-   Identify the problem.

Step Three-   Find yourself a course of action to attack it,

Step Four-   Give yourself the time to heal.

Step Five-   Stick with the plan.

~My Process~

There were many times because I didn't have a plan, that I found myself going around the same mountain. Suicidal thoughts and drinking consumed my life. I went from one thing to another. I was a wondering. My soul was crying out for help but didn't fully understand what I was crying out for. I just knew that I was tired of repeating the same cycle; the cycle of life that seemed to be filled with many defeats but very few wins. This was a constant battle and still is. I had to relearn how to think and how to live. I had to change my negative mindset and take myself out of negative situations. I had to replace those things with things that were positive. I had to stop relying on my crutches of alcohol and food. I could no longer participate in emotional drinking and eating. In 2012, I was at my heaviest; 363 lbs. I wasn't happy with myself and it showed inside and out. I had to do a complete makeover. I had to learn how to forgive those who hurt me and when unforgiveness rears its ugly head, I have to remind it that it isn't worth it. Letting go was the best thing I could do for myself. I made a list of all the things that I knew were hindering me and I prayed and asked God to reveal to me those hidden things that I was trying to hold on to. One by one, I attacked each situation. I had to learn to pray with a passion for those who hurt me. I had to ask God to forgive me and them. We both were in sin. They performed the act and I performed the act of holding onto it. I had to be quick about releasing people. The more I found myself forgiving and letting go the better my physical health became. I have lost a total of 93 lbs. My pain began to have purpose and the more purpose that it has the more I stripped the enemy of its power over my life. Every time I run into someone who has gone through something that I have went through, I am able to empower them to go on. I am able to tell them that if He did it for me He will do it for them. The more I let go the easier it became to trust God even in the midst of tribulations. I constantly remind myself He is God and He is Able. He is my Lover, my Friend, my Great I AM. HE IS my God and because I am His child and He has such a great love for me, that He saw it fit to protect my mind, body, and soul until I caught up with His Plan. I love Him and each day I sat out to fall in love with Him all over again. I can see the beauty of the world because I found it in His Love.

This is the end of this book but not to reinventing yourself in God. I pray that through my openness you have been able to see some areas in your life that you need to change so that you too can be free. Regardless of how you got here, you are here and you are here with PURPOSE. When you are overwhelmed by the hurt and pain of what has happened to you, it seems as though your life has no purpose. I was stuck in my mental wheelchair but now I AM FREE. It is a fight to stay FREE because the enemy loves for us to be bound. The more bound we are, the more we will acknowledge him instead of the Father. However. I thank GOD for GRACE and MERCY. It has covered you because you haven't tapped into your purpose. When the serpent came after Eve, the first thing he asked was, "What did God say?' The enemy isn't after your tangible things like money, family, or cars. He is after the words that God has spoken over your life before you were formed in your mother's womb.

He has a sneak preview of your life. He doesn't know the outcome. He just knows that if you tap into the true purpose that God has created for you, you will wreak havoc to his kingdom. The best part about God is that He uses every aspect of our lives to work it out for OUR GOOD. So even in your worst state, God is going to work things out for your GOOD. This is why I love this man so. He is constantly reworking what the enemy has meant for evil, FOR MY GOOD! That is the kind of God that I serve!

I pray that is also the God that you serve. If not please join me as we recite the

Sinner's prayer:

I acknowledge to You that I am a sinner, and I am sorry for my sins and the life that I have lived; I need your forgiveness.

I believe that your only begotten Son Jesus Christ shed His precious blood on the cross at Calvary and died for my sins, and I am now willing to turn from my sin.

You said in Your Holy Word, Romans 10:9 that if we confess the Lord our God and believe in our hearts that God raised Jesus from the dead, we shall be saved.

Right now I confess Jesus as the Lord of my soul. With my heart, I believe that God raised Jesus from the dead. This very moment I accept Jesus Christ as my own personal Savior and according to His Word, right now I am saved.

Know that God loves you and that it is His ultimate plan for you to have the best.

~Prayer~

God I thank you for being the God that forgives and that you are not like man who may say, "I will forgive but never forget." You forget and you still love us with a love beyond measure. I thank you for giving every reader the insight and the knowledge to know each and every situation that may be causing strong holds in their lives. I declare and decree that every yoke of bondage that has been trying to conquer them is now broken and they are being renewed and refreshed in you and that the enemy no longer has an effect on them and their lives; that every breeched area is being shown to them. That they will stand in the holy boldness that they were created for and know that you have called them. The Spirit of Shame has no place and I thank you and praise you that you that you are creating in them a new heart; a heart that will no longer be hardened. They shall go and be everything that you have called them to be; for you are Lord of lords and King of kings and that at the name of Jesus every knee shall bow and every tongue shall confess that Jesus is Lord. In Jesus' name every one of our strong holds has to bow, we sever the ties that bind us to man and not to you. Dreams and visions shall overtake them and they shall see the future, write it out and make it plain and stand on it. In Jesus' name I pray. Amen.

May the Peace and the favor of God be on you like never before!

www.ingramcontent.com/pod-product-compliance
Lightning Source LLC
Chambersburg PA
CBHW060424050426
42449CB00009B/2128